MW01098638

23870 NW West Union **Road**
Hillsboro, Oregon 97124

Georgia

by Jody Sullivan

Consultant:
Edwin Jackson
Senior Public Service Associate
Carl Vinson Institute
of Government

Capstone
press®

Mankato, Minnesota

Capstone Press
151 Good Counsel Drive • P.O. Box 669 • Mankato, Minnesota 56002
http://www.capstone-press.com
Copyright © 2003 by Capstone Press. All rights reserved.

For information regarding permission, write to Capstone Press,
151 Good Counsel Drive, P.O. Box 669, Dept. R, Mankato, Minnesota 56002.
Printed in the United States of America

Library of Congress Cataloging-in-Publication Data
Sullivan, Jody.
    Georgia / by Jody Sullivan.
    v. cm.—(Land of liberty)
    Includes bibliographical references and index.
    Contents: About Georgia—Land, climate and wildlife—History of Georgia—
Government and politics—Economy and resources—People and culture—
Timeline—State seal and flag.
    ISBN-13: 978-0-7368-1578-9 (hardcover)
    ISBN-10: 0-7368-1578-3 (hardcover)
    1. Georgia—Juvenile literature. [1. Georgia.] I. Title. II. Series.
F286.3 .S85 2003
917.58—dc21   2002010320

Summary: An introduction to the geography, history, government, politics,
    economy, resources, people, and culture of Georgia, including maps, charts,
    and a recipe.

Editorial Credits

Bradley P. Hoehn and Christopher Harbo, editors; Jennifer Schonborn, series
    and book designer; Angi Gahler, illustrator; Kelly Garvin, photo researcher;
    Eric Kudalis, product planning editor

Photo Credits

Cover images: Atlanta, Georgia, Houserstock/Dave G. Houser; peaches,
    Corbis/Richard Gross

Capstone Press/Gary Sundermeyer, 54; Corbis/AFP, 50–51; Corbis/Bettmann, 22,
25, 29; Corbis/David Muench, 8; Corbis/Gary W. Carter, 17; Corbis/Kevin
    ̣leming, 32, 44–45, 52, 53; Corbis/PACHA, 41; Corbis/Ron Austing/Frank Lane
    ̣tures Agency, 56; Digital Stock/Marty Snyderman, 16; Georgia Department of
    ̣stry, Trade & Tourism, 1, 4, 31, 37, 38, 43, 48, 57, 63; Houserstock/Dave G.
    ̣r, 40; Hulton Archive by Getty Images, 18, 26–27, 30, 36, 58; James P.
    ̣15; North Wind Picture Archives/Nancy Carter, 21; One Mile Up, Inc.,
    ̣ Pat and Chuck Blackley, 12–13; Unicorn Stock Photos/Mark E.
    ̣ U.S. Postal Service, 59

    ̣ts
    ̣Stock, Earthstar Stock, Inc., Georgia Department of Industry,
    ̣PhotoDisc, Inc.

̣ 07 06 05 04 03

Table of Contents

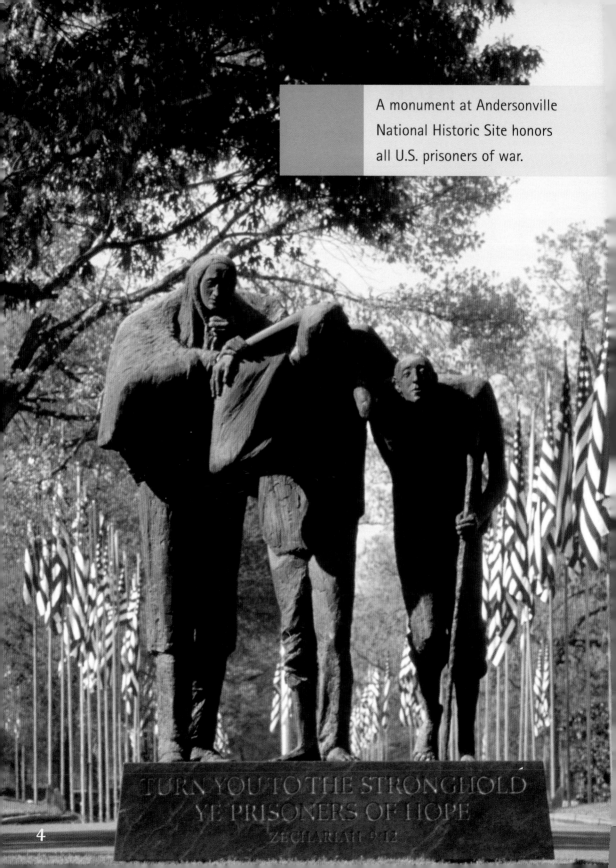

A monument at Andersonville National Historic Site honors all U.S. prisoners of war.

TURN YOU TO THE STRONGHOLD
YE PRISONERS OF HOPE
ZECHARIAH 9:12

Chapter 1

About Georgia

Andersonville was one of the largest Confederate
military prisons built during the Civil War. Built in 1864,
Andersonville was known as Camp Sumter. The prison was
open for 14 months. More than 45,000 Union soldiers were
held there. Almost 13,000 of the prisoners died from bad
water, dirty conditions, or a lack of shelter and food.

Andersonville is the only national site to serve as a
memorial to all U.S. prisoners of war. On October 16, 1970,
it was made a national historic site. The 495-acre (200-hectare)
park includes the prison site and a national cemetery.

The Peach State

One of the oldest states, Georgia is rich in history and natural beauty. Events that shaped the state and country are preserved in Georgia. Long ago, Creek and Cherokee Indians roamed the land. Two wars took place in Georgia. Georgia is also the birthplace of the Civil Rights movement.

Georgia has been an important state in U.S. history. It was one of the 13 original states. In January 1788, Georgia became the fourth state to vote for the new U.S. Constitution.

Georgia is located in the southeastern part of the United States. This region is often called the Deep South. Tennessee and North Carolina border Georgia to the north. Alabama lies to the west. Florida shares Georgia's southern border. South Carolina and the Atlantic Ocean lie to the east of Georgia.

Georgia's nickname is the Peach State. Georgia peaches are famous for their flavor. Peach orchards in Georgia harvest more than 100 million pounds (45 million kilograms) of peaches each year. In 1995, the peach became Georgia's state fruit.

Georgia Cities

NORTH CAROLINA

TENNESSEE

SOUTH CAROLINA

• Rome

Chattahoochee River

• Gainesville

• Athens

⊛ Atlanta

Savannah River

Augusta

• La Grange

• Macon

GEORGIA

Savannah

ALABAMA

• Columbus

○ Andersonville
National Historic Site

ATLANTIC
OCEAN

• Albany

• Valdosta

FLORIDA

Legend

⊛ Capital

• City

○ Point of Interest

～ River

20   40   60   80   100
40   60   80   100
ters

N

W   E

S

*Gulf of
Mexico*

7

People can visit High Falls in northern Georgia's Blue Ridge Mountains.

Chapter 2

Land, Climate, and Wildlife

Georgia has five natural regions. These regions are the Coastal Plain, the Piedmont Plateau, the Blue Ridge, the Ridge and Valley, and the Appalachian Plateau. The Coastal Plain is a lowland area. The four other regions are higher in elevation than the plain.

Coastal Plain

The Coastal Plain covers about 60 percent of Georgia. It is mostly flat, but gradually rises to a height of nearly 800 feet (240 meters) above sea level near the Fall Line. This group of waterfalls and river rapids formed where hard rock meets softer rock. Large salt marshes and freshwater swamps lie in the plain. The Okefenokee Swamp covers the southeastern corner of Georgia. The swamp stretches from the Coastal Plain to northern Florida.

Georgia's coastline is about 100 miles (160 kilometers) long. Bays and river mouths mark the Atlantic coastline. A chain of sea islands is separated from the mainland by a narrow waterway.

Plateaus, Ridges, and Valleys

The Piedmont Plateau covers about 30 percent of Georgia. It lies between the Coastal Plain and the higher Appalachian land. Rolling hills cover the Piedmont. The gently sloping areas of the Piedmont are farmed. Forests cover the more hilly sections.

The Blue Ridge region includes the Blue Ridge Mountains and the neighboring valley. This region makes up only about 5 percent of the state. Brasstown Bald is the highest point in Georgia. This mountain rises 4,784 feet (1,458 meters) above

Georgia's Land Features

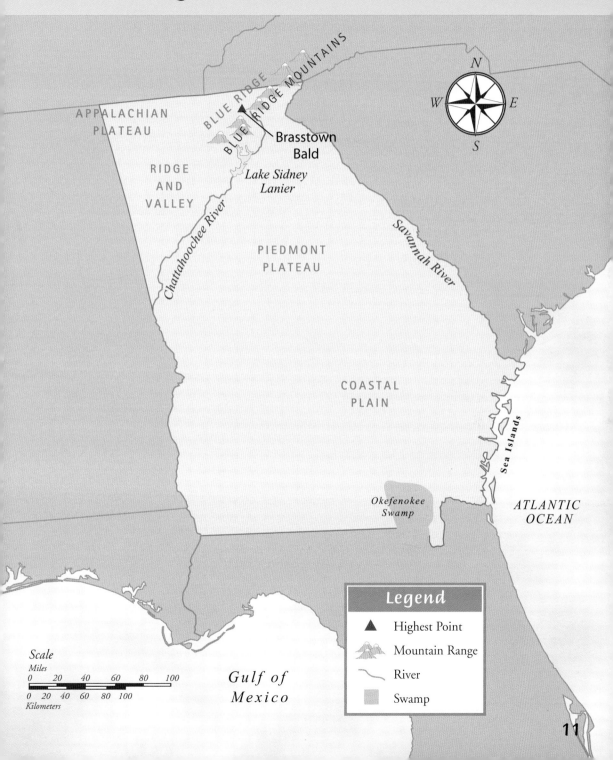

APPALACHIAN
PLATEAU

BLUE RIDGE

BLUE RIDGE MOUNTAINS

BLUE RIDGE

▲ Brasstown
Bald

RIDGE
AND
VALLEY

*Lake Sidney
Lanier*

Chattahoochee River

PIEDMONT
PLATEAU

Savannah River

COASTAL
PLAIN

Sea Islands

*Okefenokee
Swamp*

ATLANTIC
OCEAN

N
W   E
S

Scale
Miles
0   20   40   60   80   100

0   20   40   60   80   100
Kilometers

*Gulf of
Mexico*

Legend

▲	Highest Point
🏔	Mountain Range
∿	River
▨	Swamp

sea level. The Blue Ridge region also has many forests, deep river valleys, and small waterfalls.

Tall ridges and narrow valleys stretch across the Ridge and Valley region of northwestern Georgia. Most of the forested ridges reach heights of about 1,500 feet (460 meters). People farm the land in the valleys.

The Appalachian Plateau is in Georgia's northwestern corner. Many birch, oak, and beech trees cover these low mountains.

Rivers and Lakes

Georgia has 71,000 miles (11,400 kilometers) of rivers and streams. The Savannah is the longest river in Georgia. In the eastern part of the Coastal Plain, rivers flow east toward the Atlantic Ocean. Rivers in the western half flow south to the Gulf of Mexico. Only a few rivers in Georgia flow north to the Tennessee River.

Most of Georgia's large lakes were made by people. Utility companies built some lakes for generating power. Other lakes

The long, green canyons of Cloudland Canyon State Park are part of Georgia's Appalachian Plateau.

were made to control floods. Lake Sidney Lanier is on the Chattahoochee River. It covers 72 square miles (186 square kilometers). It is the largest lake within the state.

Climate

Georgia's regions have different climates. The Coastal Plain and much of the Piedmont have hot summers and mild winters. Humidity is usually high throughout the year. In the mountains, temperatures are much cooler.

Georgia receives more than half of its yearly rainfall during the spring and summer. Each year, Georgia receives between 46 and 76 inches (116 and 193 centimeters) of rainfall and snowfall combined.

Plant Life

Forests and woodlands cover about 60 percent of Georgia. Most of Georgia's mountain ranges are covered with trees. Ash, beech, and hickory trees grow in the mountains. The live oak, Georgia's state tree, is common along the Atlantic coast.

Alligators swim among the lily pads in the Okefenokee Swamp.

Okefenokee Swamp is a large wilderness of marshlands. The wet climate is perfect for green lily pads, wild orchids, bald cypress trees, and Spanish moss.

Flowering plants grow well in Georgia. The Cherokee rose, the state flower, grows in many parts of the state. Shrubs and small flowering trees, such as laurel and flowering dogwood, also are common in Georgia.

Manatees

Manatees are most commonly found in the coastal rivers and bays of Georgia and Florida. These warm-water mammals sometimes weigh as much as 3,000 pounds (1,360 kilograms). Manatees swim south when temperatures drop in winter.

Manatees are in danger of dying out. Scientists believe only about 3,000 manatees still live in the wild. Speeding boats, jet skis, and other watercraft kill more than 100 slow-swimming manatees each year.

Wetlands and Wildlife

Georgia's coastal and wetland areas are home to about 75 kinds of freshwater fish and about 20 kinds of saltwater fish. Shrimp, crabs, and oysters are also found along the coastal regions. Mountain trout, bass, and catfish swim in the lakes and rivers of northern and central Georgia.

About 80 types of amphibians and 80 types of reptiles live in Georgia. Georgia's largest reptile, the alligator, lives in the state's swamps. Water moccasins, timber rattlesnakes, and other venomous snakes are found in Georgia.

About 300 kinds of birds live in Georgia. Many birds from the northern United States and Canada spend the winter in Georgia. The brown thrasher is Georgia's state bird. Ten of the state's birds are in danger of dying out. The red-cockaded woodpecker has been listed as an endangered species since 1968. It lives throughout southern Georgia.

Many mammals make their homes in Georgia. Black bears live in the northern mountains and the Okefenokee Swamp. Bobcats roam Georgia's rural areas. Red foxes, opossums, flying squirrels, and raccoons make their homes in forested areas across the state.

Water moccasins are venomous snakes that live in Georgia's swamps and wetlands.

Spanish explorer Hernando de Soto was one of the first Europeans to arrive in Georgia.

Chapter 3

History of Georgia

In the 1500s, more than 1 million native people lived in the southeastern United States. At that time, Georgia's native people were called the Mississippian Indians.

Spanish explorers were the first Europeans to visit Georgia. In 1540, Hernando de Soto and other explorers arrived in Georgia. They carried smallpox, measles, and other diseases with them. These diseases killed most of the Mississippian Indians. Those who survived adopted new lifestyles and broke into small tribes. Later, they became known as the Creek and Cherokee Indians.

The Spanish called the land Guale. In the mid-1590s, Franciscan friars and priests from Spain built missions in

Did you know...?
The First African Baptist Church was the first African American church in the United States. It was founded in Savannah in 1788.

Guale. They wanted to bring the Catholic religion to the New World.

English Colonization

England questioned Spain's claim to Guale. In 1670, English settlers in Charleston, South Carolina, began to move south. In 1680, 300 Indians, who were working with the English, attacked the Spanish missions and outposts. They forced the Spanish off the land. By 1685, the Spanish left Guale and went to Florida.

In 1732, King George II of England created a new colony. He named the colony Georgia. James E. Oglethorpe and others were in charge of this colony. In 1733, Oglethorpe brought more than 100 colonists to Georgia. They set up the town of Savannah. Oglethorpe also founded Augusta in 1736.

New Settlement

For the next 20 years, people from Europe continued to arrive in Georgia. Most of these people wanted religious freedom. Oglethorpe and other leaders wanted a society in which no one was rich or poor. The leaders gave settlers land and supplies.

In 1736, James Oglethorpe founded Fort Frederica on Saint Simons Island to protect his settlements from Spanish attack.

Colonists had to work hard to support themselves. Georgia was the only colony to have laws against alcohol and slavery.

The farmers in Georgia complained they could not compete with the crop prices of other colonies that allowed slavery. Georgians wanted to have slaves to work in their fields. Oglethorpe argued that slaves would make settlers lazy and that slavery was wrong. The settlers won the argument.

By 1750, slavery was legal in Georgia. A plantation system developed based on slavery.

In 1752, Georgia became a royal colony. Representatives of the king of England led the colony. The number of colonists grew from about 5,000 to 40,000 from 1750 to 1776. African slaves made up half of Georgia's population.

The American Revolution

During the mid-1700s, Georgia needed Great Britain's money and protection. Many Georgians believed that British rule was

Slaves picked cotton on plantations during the 1700s and 1800s. These slaves worked on a plantation near Savannah, Georgia, in the 1860s.

Did you know...?
George Walton, Lyman Hall, and Button Gwinnett were the three Georgians to sign the Declaration of Independence in 1776.

good for their society. In the 1760s, some Georgians began resisting British taxes. When the Revolutionary War (1775–1783) began, many people in Georgia felt the need to separate from Britain.

In 1776, three Georgian leaders were among those who signed the Declaration of Independence. The same year, Georgia created a plan for government called Rules and Regulations. In 1777, Georgia adopted a new state constitution. On January 2, 1788, Georgia was the fourth state to adopt the U.S. Constitution.

Thousands of settlers from nearby states moved to Georgia. Between 1790 and 1810, the state's population tripled.

Taking of Native Lands

As more settlers moved into Georgia, U.S. treaties with Creek and Cherokee Indians were broken. In 1825, Governor George Troup threatened to remove the Creek by force. By 1827, the Creek turned over their remaining lands in Georgia. They moved west to Indian Territory in present-day Oklahoma.

In 1828, gold was discovered on Cherokee land in northern Georgia. People rushed to the gold fields. The government held a lottery in 1832 to give Cherokee lands to white citizens.

In 1835, a group of Cherokee signed away their lands. According to the Treaty of New Echota, the Cherokee had to move west to Indian Territory. They refused to go. In 1838, the federal government forced them to march west. This march was called the "Trail of Tears" because thousands of Cherokee died during the long walk.

The Civil War

By the 1850s, slavery divided the United States. Some Southerners wanted to break away from the Union. They feared some members of government would try to get rid of slavery or stop its expansion in the West.

In 1860, the election of Abraham Lincoln as president pushed South Carolina to break away from the United States. Lincoln was a member of the new Republican Party. Southern democratic leaders believed his party was against slavery. In 1861, Georgia joined South Carolina and other Southern states

The Battle of Chickamauga was the first Civil War battle fought in Georgia. Almost 35,000 soldiers died during the two-day battle.

in forming the Confederate States of America. The Civil War (1861–1865) had begun.

During the Civil War, many battles were fought in Georgia. The first major battle in Georgia was in September 1863. The Union Army was turned back at the Battle of Chickamauga.

In spring 1864, a Union force led by General William T. Sherman attacked Georgia. Sherman and his men captured

Atlanta in September. Confederate soldiers set fire to the city to stop Sherman's troops from using their supplies. Sherman captured Savannah in December. He then marched north to South Carolina. In April 1865, General Robert E. Lee surrendered the main Confederate forces.

The Civil War changed Georgia forever. The war brought an end to slavery. The end of slavery and the destruction of factories and crops wiped out much of the South's economy.

Reconstruction

Reconstruction of the South started after the Civil War and continued until 1877. President Andrew Johnson worked to build state governments and readmit the states to the Union. In 1870, Georgia rejoined the Union.

Georgia's economy started to improve. People started new banks and businesses. The cotton textile industry grew and natural resources were developed. In 1868, Atlanta became

Many of Atlanta's buildings were damaged or destroyed by the Confederate Army near the end of the Civil War.

"I have a dream that my four little children will one day live in a nation where they will not be judged by the color of their skin but by the content of their character."

—Martin Luther King Jr.

the new state capital. Atlanta soon grew into Georgia's main manufacturing center.

Georgia in the Early 1900s

During World War I (1914–1918), Georgia supplied the United States with much needed farm products. By the 1920s, Georgia farmers were suffering great losses. An insect called the boll weevil destroyed much of the cotton crop. Many farm workers left farms and moved to cities and towns.

The Great Depression (1929–1939) made life in Georgia even harder. Georgia was one of the poorest states. An average Georgia family earned only about half as much money as families in other states.

World War II (1939–1945) brought economic help to Georgia. Military bases were built and many jobs were created. The U.S. government also hired Georgia businesses to build airplanes, ships, and supplies for the war. The war brought many northern businesses south to Georgia.

The Civil Rights Movement

The Civil Rights movement of the 1950s and 1960s was centered in Atlanta. Civil rights leader Martin Luther King Jr. lived in Atlanta. African Americans had voting rights, but they were still not equal to whites. African Americans had to use separate restaurants, schools, churches, restrooms, and even drinking fountains.

In 1960, African American college students in Atlanta and other Georgia cities began to protest. They held peaceful protests at segregated restaurants, parks, and churches. They

In the 1950s, segregation forced African American children to go to different schools than white children.

marched, picketed, and avoided stores. King became a powerful voice in the fight for civil rights.

In 1964, Congress passed the Civil Rights Act. The act made segregation and discrimination of any kind illegal. Many Georgia politicians and citizens were against the act. In 1971, Democrat Jimmy Carter became governor of Georgia. Carter wanted equal rights and equal opportunity for all. He was elected president of the United States five years later.

Martin Luther King Jr. was a powerful leader during the Civil Rights movement.

Visitors to the World of Coca-Cola museum in Atlanta learn the history of this soft drink made in Georgia.

Recent Years

Georgia's population and economy has grown more rapidly than those of most states. Between 1975 and 2000, Georgia was the fifth fastest growing state in the country. Many people began moving to Georgia because of its growing industries and job opportunities. Atlanta-based companies such as Coca-Cola, United Parcel Service, and Home Depot have helped Georgia grow.

Construction on Georgia's capitol began in 1884. The building was completed in 1889.

Chapter 4

Government and Politics

Politics have played an important part in Georgia's history. The Democratic Party controlled politics in the state from about 1870 until the 1960s. Since then, many Republicans have moved to Georgia from other states. A number of Georgians who grew up as Democrats have become Republicans. Many things changed as the Republican Party gained power. Republicans favor lower taxes and limits on federal government control.

"I say to you quite frankly that the time for racial discrimination is over. Our people have already made this major and difficult decision, but we cannot underestimate the challenge of hundreds of minor decisions yet to be made."

—President Jimmy Carter, in his inaugural address, 1977

In the 1970s, African Americans began to gain power. In 1972, Andrew Young became the state's first African American member of Congress since Reconstruction. Young was elected from a district with a white majority. President Jimmy Carter appointed Young to represent the United States at the United Nations.

Branches of Government

Georgia's state government has executive, legislative, and judicial branches. The governor leads the executive branch. Georgia's governor serves a four-year term. Each governor can serve no more than two terms in a row.

Georgia's state legislature is called the General Assembly. The assembly has 56 senators and 180 representatives. They meet every year in Atlanta for 40 days, starting on the second Monday in January.

Georgia's State Government

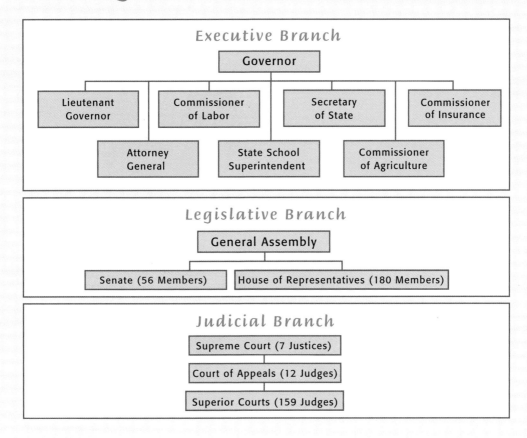

Executive Branch

Governor

Lieutenant Governor | Commissioner of Labor | Secretary of State | Commissioner of Insurance

Attorney General | State School Superintendent | Commissioner of Agriculture

Legislative Branch

General Assembly

Senate (56 Members) | House of Representatives (180 Members)

Judicial Branch

Supreme Court (7 Justices)

Court of Appeals (12 Judges)

Superior Courts (159 Judges)

The Supreme Court of Georgia is the highest court in Georgia's judicial branch. It is the final court of appeal in most cases. Seven justices serve on the supreme court. They are elected for six-year terms. The justices elect one of their members to be the chief justice.

Jimmy Carter

Jimmy Carter is one of Georgia's most famous politicians. Born on October 1, 1924, James Earl Carter Jr. grew up on his family's peanut farm in Plains, Georgia. In 1946, Carter graduated from the Naval Academy in Annapolis, Maryland. In 1962, he entered state politics. He was elected governor of Georgia in 1970.

In 1976, Carter ran for president of the United States. Carter and his running mate, Senator Walter F. Mondale of Minnesota, defeated President Gerald R. Ford.

During his presidency, Carter fought economic problems. He helped to create jobs for nearly 8 million people and to lower the federal budget. He created the Department of Education and tried to fix the Social Security system.

Since his presidency, Carter has worked to improve human rights and find peaceful solutions to international conflicts. In 2002, Jimmy Carter won the Nobel Peace Prize for his peace efforts.

West Union School
23870 NW West Union Road
Hillsboro, Oregon 97124

Georgia Schools

The state constitution of 1777 provided for state-funded schools in each county. A state school system did not develop until 1872. At first, only elementary schools and state universities were supported by the state. High schools were included in 1912. Today, school attendance is required for children ages 7 through 16.

In the 1990s, Georgia spent about $4,170 per year on each student's education. The national average is $5,310. Class sizes in Georgia's schools are larger than the national average.

Students learn about snakes on a field trip to Oxbow Meadows Environmental Learning Center in Columbus, Georgia.

Workers make thread, fabric, clothing, and carpet in Georgia's textile factories.

Chapter 5

Economy and Resources

During the 1700s, Georgia's major plantation crops were rice, sugarcane, and a blue dye called indigo. When cotton was introduced in 1786, it became the most important crop. In the 1920s, boll weevils destroyed many of the South's cotton crops. Gradually, Georgia's other industries became more important to the state's economy.

Economic Growth

In the 1830s, the textile industry developed in Georgia. Manufacturing became even more important after the

Civil War. The manufacture of war supplies during World War II further increased the business.

World War II brought more changes to Georgia's economy. New military bases were built. The bases brought jobs with better pay. The U.S. government provided money to build airplanes, ships, and weapons for the war effort.

Georgia's transportation business grew rapidly in the 1950s. Today, shipping and travel are key to Georgia's economic development.

Georgia industries ship textiles, lumber, and other products to many countries around the world.

Ted Turner

Atlanta resident Ted Turner is a business leader known for his TV networks and movie studios. In 1970, Turner bought his first TV station in Atlanta. In 1980, Turner started Cable News Network (CNN). CNN was the first 24-hour TV news station. In the 1990s, Turner bought several movie studios, including Castle Rock and New Line Cinema.

Turner loves sports. He bought the Atlanta Braves baseball team in 1975. In 1977, he bought the Atlanta Hawks basketball team. Turner started the Goodwill Games in 1986. This international sports competition is held every four years. In 1997, Turner started the Atlanta Thrashers pro hockey team.

Manufacturing

Manufacturing brings in more money and jobs than any other business in Georgia. Textiles are Georgia's top manufactured products. Georgia textiles include velvet, denim, carpet, and wool.

Did you know...?
One 500-pound
(227-kilogram) bale
of cotton can produce
242 pairs of jeans, 690
bath towels, or 3,085
cloth diapers.

The manufacture of cars and airplanes also is important to Georgia. The Atlanta area has two automobile plants. The large Lockheed Martin aircraft plant in Marietta makes jets for the U.S. Air Force.

Food processing is another important business in Georgia. Gainesville has one of the world's leading poultry processing centers. Brunswick is a center for canning and freezing seafood and vegetables.

Agriculture and Fishing

Once Georgia's main industry, agriculture now ranks second to the manufacturing industry. In the 1990s, Georgia had 43,000 farms. Today, about 60 percent of the state's total farm income comes from the sale of livestock and livestock products. Poultry is Georgia's chief farm product.

Several crops provide the rest of Georgia's farm income. Peanuts are Georgia's chief crop. The state leads the nation in growing peanuts. Cotton was Georgia's leading crop for

Georgia grows almost half of the U.S. peanut crop each year. Peanuts are harvested each September or October.

many years. Cotton grows on the Coastal Plain and the Piedmont Plateau. Peaches are Georgia's main fruit crop. They grow near Macon and Fort Valley. Georgia's other important crops include watermelons, pecans, corn, tobacco, and soybeans.

Compared to other coastal states, Georgia has a small commercial fishing business. Seafood harvested in Georgia's waters includes shrimp, crab, and oysters.

Natural Resources and Mining

Natural resources are an important part of Georgia's economy. Georgia is a leading supplier of lumber and wood pulp products. Most lumber comes from pine trees. Many fields that were once used to grow cotton are now forested.

Georgia produces several minerals of national importance. Clay and stone are Georgia's most valuable minerals. Georgia ranks first among the states in kaolin and marble production, and second in granite. Kaolin is a white clay used to make paper, paint, plastics, rubber, and many other products. Georgia marble is a popular material used for buildings and gravestones. Georgia also is among the country's leading producers of ocher and fuller's earth. Both products are used to make vegetable and mineral oils.

Georgia's lumber mills process pine and hardwood trees. The trees are cut into lumber and made into other wood products.

On hot days, children play in the fountain at Atlanta's Centennial Olympic Park.

Chapter 6

People and Culture

Many Georgians descended from British, German, Austrian, and Swiss settlers. Most of these people settled along the coast. People came to northern Georgia mainly from North Carolina, Virginia, and Pennsylvania. These residents were mostly Scottish and Irish.

In 1860, nearly half of Georgia's population was African American. Almost all of them were slaves. They lived on plantations in the Coastal Plain and the Piedmont Plateau. After the Civil War, some African Americans moved to northern cities. In the 1970s, many African Americans returned to Georgia looking for good jobs.

More than half of Georgia's population lives within 60 miles (97 kilometers) of Atlanta. Columbus, Savannah, and Augusta are other major cities. Savannah is the oldest city in Georgia. It was the largest city until the growth of Atlanta in the 1900s. Rural areas in Georgia are lightly populated.

As a southern state, Georgia is thought to have tradition, culture, and charm. The term "southern hospitality" is a common expression. It means southerners are generally kind and generous to strangers.

The Atlanta Ballet was founded by Dorothy Alexander in the 1930s. It is the oldest professional dance company in the United States.

Georgia's Ethnic Background

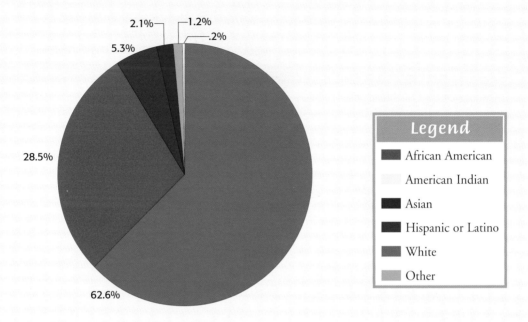

2.1% 1.2%
5.3% .2%
28.5%
62.6%

Legend
- African American
- American Indian
- Asian
- Hispanic or Latino
- White
- Other

Atlanta is Georgia's cultural center. People visit Atlanta to enjoy art, theater, and music. The Atlanta Symphony Orchestra is one of the South's leading orchestras. The Atlanta Ballet performs at the Atlanta Civic Center.

Food

Georgians enjoy a wide variety of southern food. Grits are popular in Georgia. Grits are made with corn or hominy. They are cooked with water or milk. People eat grits as hot cereal or served as a side dish.

Georgians are known for other original recipes. Hush puppies are popular in Georgia. These cornmeal dumplings are deep-fried and served hot. For dessert, Georgians enjoy sweet potato pie and pecan pie.

Sports and Entertainment

Atlanta is home to several pro sports teams. These include the NFL's Falcons, the Braves baseball team, the Thrashers hockey team, and the NBA's Hawks. Atlanta hosted the 1996 Summer Olympic Games. The Olympic Stadium is now the home

of the Braves. One of the most famous golf events in the United States, the Masters Tournament, is held every April in Augusta.

Georgia has often been the subject of films and books. One of the most popular films of all time is *Gone With the Wind*. This film was released in 1939. The film is based on a novel by Georgia-born author Margaret Mitchell. The film and novel tell the story of the Civil War and Reconstruction era from the South's point of view. *Gone With the Wind* received several Oscars.

The Atlanta Falcons joined the NFL in 1965. Today, the Falcons play their regular season games in the Georgia Dome.

Plantation Homes

Georgia is known for its plantation homes. These homes were usually unpainted, two story homes. On wealthy plantations, the homes sometimes had tall, Greek-style columns and covered porches. Plantation homes were built before the Civil War.

Georgia is also the subject of a rhythm and blues song called "Georgia on My Mind." Stuart Gorrell and Hoagy Carmichael wrote the song. It was made popular by singer and pianist Ray Charles. "Georgia on My Mind" is Georgia's state song.

State Events and Holidays

Georgia celebrates many holidays to honor its history. Martin Luther King Jr. Day is a national holiday observed on the third Monday of January. Many Georgians do volunteer work on this day. February 12 is Georgia Day. This holiday celebrates the anniversary of the founding of Savannah in 1733.

Georgia festivals are held throughout the year. Some of the state's important events include Riverfest Weekend in

Columbus in April and the Andersonville Historic Fair in May. The Big Pig Jig takes place in Vienna each October. This festival honors barbecue cooking.

Georgia's natural beauty and southern culture welcome thousands of people to the state each year. From Andersonville to the Okefenokee Swamp, the Peach State shows visitors an important part of America's history.

People watch reenactments of Civil War battles during the Andersonville Historic Fair.

Recipe: Peach Cobbler

As the Peach State, Georgia is famous for delicious peaches. Peach cobbler is a tasty dessert that many Georgians enjoy.

Ingredients

4 to 6 cups (960 to 1,440 mL) canned sliced peaches, drained
¼ cup (60 mL) sugar
1 teaspoon (5 mL) cinnamon
1 teaspoon (5 mL) nutmeg
1 large egg, beaten
1 cup (240 mL) self-rising flour
1 cup (240 mL) sugar
½ cup (120 mL) butter

Equipment

9- by 13-inch (23- by 33-centimeter) baking pan
mixing bowl
measuring spoons
mixing spoon
dry-ingredient measuring cups
fork
small bowl for melting butter

What You Do

1. Preheat the oven to 350º F (180º C).

2. Place the peaches in the bottom of the baking pan.

3. Sprinkle ¼ cup (60 mL) sugar, cinnamon, and nutmeg on sliced peaches.

4. Stir together, making sure bottom of pan is covered with peach mixture.

5. In a mixing bowl, mix egg, flour, and 1 cup (240 mL) of sugar into a crumb-like mixture with a fork.

6. Cover the peaches with the crumb mixture.

7. Melt butter in a small bowl in a microwave and drizzle over crumb topping.

8. Bake for 30 minutes at 350º F (180º C) or until top turns slightly brown and crusty.

9. Serve either hot or cold. Can be served with ice cream.

Makes 8–10 servings

Georgia's Flag and Seal

Georgia's Flag

Georgia's current flag was adopted in 2001. The flag shows the state seal in gold on a field of blue. Thirteen white stars surround the seal. A gold ribbon is under the seal. The ribbon has small images of the three Georgia state flags from the past, as well as the current and first versions of the U.S. flag.

Georgia's State Seal

The Great Seal of Georgia was adopted in 1799. On its front side are three pillars supporting an arch. The pillars represent the three branches of government. A man stands with a drawn sword. He is protecting the Constitution, whose principles are wisdom, justice, and moderation. The year 1776 represents the Declaration of Independence. The other side of the seal shows a ship with cotton and tobacco and a man plowing.

Almanac

General Facts

Nickname: Peach State

Population: 8,186,453
(U.S. Census 2000)
Population rank: 10th

Capital: Atlanta

Largest cities: Atlanta,
Augusta, Columbus,
Savannah, Athens

Agricultural products:
Peanuts, poultry, tobacco,
corn, cotton, soybeans,
eggs, peaches

Agriculture

Average summer
temperature:
79 degrees Fahrenheit
(26 degrees Celsius)

Average winter
temperature:
48 degrees Fahrenheit
(9 degrees Celsius)

Average annual
precipitation: 50 inches
(127 centimeters)

Climate

Area: 59,441 square miles
(153,952 square kilometers)
Size rank: 24th

Highest point: Brasstown
Bald Mountain, 4,784 feet
(1,458 meters) above sea level

Lowest point: Atlantic coast,
sea level

Geography

Brown thrasher

Cherokee rose

Bird: Brown thrasher

Dance: Square dance

Flower: Cherokee rose

Fruit: Peach

Insect: Honeybee

Mammal: Right whale

Natural resources:
Lumber, granite, marble

Economy

Types of industry:
Textiles and clothes,
transportation equipment,
food processing, timber,
paper products, chemical
products, tourism

Symbols

Motto: Wisdom, justice,
and moderation

Reptile: Gopher tortoise

First governor: John A.
Treutlen

Song: "Georgia on My
Mind," words by Stuart
Gorrell and music by Hoagy
Carmichael

Statehood: January 2,
1788 (4th state)

Tree: Live oak

U.S. Representatives: 13

U.S. Senators: 2

U.S. electoral votes: 15

Government

Counties: 159

Timeline

State History

1540
Spanish explorer Hernando de Soto arrives in Georgia.

1733
James E. Oglethorpe founds Savannah.

1777
Georgia's first state constitution is adopted. John A. Treutlen is elected the first governor.

1788
Georgia becomes the fourth state to adopt the U.S. Constitution.

1861
After Lincoln's election, Georgia secedes from the Union fearing slavery will be limited or made illegal.

U.S. History

1620
Pilgrims establish the Massachusetts Bay Colony.

1775–1783
American colonies fight for independence from Great Britain in the Revolutionary War.

1812–1814
The United States fights Great Britain in the War of 1812.

1861–1865
Union states fight Confederate states in the Civil War.

1920s

The boll weevil destroys Georgia's cotton crops; the state's cotton industry declines.

1976

Former governor Jimmy Carter is elected president of the United States.

1996

Atlanta hosts the Summer Olympic Games.

1870

Georgia rejoins the Union.

1960s

Dr. Martin Luther King Jr. leads the Civil Rights Movement.

1929–1939

The United States experiences the Great Depression.

1964

U.S. Congress passes the Civil Rights Act, which makes discrimination illegal.

2001

Terrorists attack the Pentagon and the World Trade Center on September 11.

1914–1918

World War I is fought; the United States enters the war in 1917.

1939–1945

World War II is fought; the United States enters the war in 1941.

Words to Know

abolition (ab-uh-LISH-uhn)—putting an end to something; the Civil War resulted in the end of slavery.

charter (CHAR-tur)—an official document that creates a city or colony and provides for a government

endangered (en-DAYN-jurd)—at risk of dying out

plain (PLANE)—a large, flat area of land

reservoir (REZ-ur-vwar)—a natural or artificial structure that is a holding area for a large amount of water

secede (si-SEED)—to break away from a group

segregation (seg-ruh-GAY-shuhn)—the policy of separating people according to their race

textile (TEK-stile)—a fabric or cloth that is woven or knitted

Union (YOON-yuhn)—a name for the United States; during the Civil War, the Northern states were called the Union.

venomous (VEN-uh-muhss)—having or producing a poison called venom; some snakes are venomous.

wetland (WET-land)—an area covered with water for at least part of the year; wetlands include swamps, marshes, and bays.

To Learn More

Claybourne, Anna. *Martin Luther King, Jr.: Civil Rights Hero.* Famous Lives. Austin, Texas: Raintree Steck-Vaughn, 2002.

Otfiniski, Steven. *Georgia.* Celebrate the States. New York: Benchmark Books, 2001.

Robinson Masters, Nancy. *Georgia.* America the Beautiful. New York: Children's Press, 1999.

Stechschulte, Pattie. *Georgia.* From Sea to Shining Sea. New York. Children's Press, 2001.

Internet Sites

Track down many sites about Georgia.
Visit the FACT HOUND at *http://www.facthound.com*

IT IS EASY! IT IS FUN!
1) Go to *http://www.facthound.com*
2) Type in: 0736815783
3) Click on "FETCH IT" and FACT HOUND will find several links hand-picked by our editors.

Relax and let our pal FACT HOUND do the research for you!

Places to Write and Visit

Andersonville National Historic Site
496 Cemetery Road
Andersonville, GA 31711

The Carter Center
Public Information Office
453 Freedom Parkway
Atlanta, GA 30307

Georgia State Capitol
214 State Capitol
Atlanta, GA 30334

Margaret Mitchell House and Museum
990 Peachtree St.
Atlanta, GA 30309

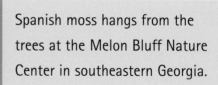

Spanish moss hangs from the trees at the Melon Bluff Nature Center in southeastern Georgia.

Index

T 57076